YOU ARE IN CHARGE OF YOUR DESTINY:

The simplest steps to achieving your Dreamed destiny

NANCY BRANDT

Table of Content

INTRODUCTION

Construct the Pillars of Your Destiny and Take Charge of Your Own Life

Do you feel disappointed with your ongoing way throughout everyday life? Is it true that you are prepared to assume complete command over your own life yet not certain where to begin?

Nancy Brandt Drive Your Destiny gives you the fortitude, certainty, and versatility to be the Captain of your destiny. This book is your finished manual for assisting you with

making anything you need in your life.

Presently you can take out the mystery and supplant vulnerability with clearness. Eliminate your self-uncertainty while expanding the fearlessness you never realized you had. Throw out your propensity for casual exercise and supplant it with monstrous activity.

In Drive Your Destiny, you will likewise gain proficiency with the particular methodologies to:

Ace the vital choices in your day-to-day existence

Change your restricting convictions with the 6-point framework

Engage your existence with strong vision-building techniques

Assume responsibility for your life by growing better propensities

Arrange life-upgrading objectives

Foster a bit-by-bit outline for building outcomes in all parts of your life

Amplify your psychological, physical, and otherworldly energy

Drive Your Destiny will train you the keys to finding the inward significance inside you. You will figure out how to assume responsibility and direct your activities to work for you rather than against you. As you will see, neither the conditions nor the outer circumstances choose your predetermination — you do.

The time has come to pursue a choice and make a huge move

towards showing the world you envision living in. Embrace the endowment of living life to the fullest and Drive Your Destiny home today.

Charter 1

How To take Charge Of Your Destiny

Each spirit comes to Earth with a pre-arranged yet adaptable plan for some random lifetime given your past blunders which should be settled and refined for your profound advancement.

Relating predetermination to luck is ordinary. Be that as it may, karma isn't in the rest of the world; it is in your discernment. Your degree of awareness decides your karma. So, fate depends

on your cognizance, which is the entirety of your viewpoints, sentiments, activities, and decisions.

Given underneath are the 10 hints on the best way to assume responsibility for your fate:

Take on a Healthy Regime: Indisciplined way of life is normally the reason for a wide range of medical conditions. You are not bound to endure ailment and infection. Man is made in the picture and resemblance of God and is intended to live as a flawless being in all immaculateness and flawlessness.

At the point when God made man, He additionally exposed him to the Law of Cause and Effect and gave to him the endowment of

the option to choose to manage his circumstances all that can be expected.

Notwithstanding, wrong decisions and the abuse of his unrestrained choice risked the existence of a man with difficulties and experiencing fate in the course of his life. Furthermore, similarly, as man accidentally made an experience in his life, he likewise can change his situation with refined contemplations, mind, and shrewdness, and in this way foreordain himself to have a more healthy existence in the future.

The way to a solid future is to stay in shape with regular exercise schedules, yoga, and contemplation, take nature strolls and move around on the planet

with heaps of uplifting outlooks. In particular, participate in unadulterated food varieties which develop and age in the sun, for ideal wellbeing. Such food varieties are a rich wellspring of pranic energy which is enabling your body, brain, and soul.

Offer Thanks: The demeanor of appreciation assists with keeping you sensitive to the Universal energies of good wellbeing and overflow. Be thankful for everything throughout everyday life - for the wealthy and the less wealthy. Each time you offer thanks, life gives you the motivation to be appreciative. At the point when you are disappointed with your life you are accidentally

fixing your destiny to flounder in hopelessness through your effort.

Center in the NOW: Your fate is in the NOW. Your past and future are non-existent; there is no harmony and bliss in these illusionary timetables. Your previous makes you dismal while what's in store fills you with nervousness and stress. Your existence is at the time where everlasting harmony wins. So live in the everlasting second; this is where you can wind around the strings of your fate for a blissful, productive life.

Be Resilient: Move with the River of Life. Opposition causes a lot of languishing. Come calmly with the progressions throughout everyday

life or the power of the tide will whip and hit you as it surges along its course. Would it be a good idea for you to attempt to oppose the stream? The Tides of Time are no respecter of man. Permit the River of Life to convey you securely to the radiant shores of your pre-ordained objective.

Practice Meditation: Refine your psyche with day-to-day reflection and innovative representation. Contemplation assists with honing your concentration, and cleans up your brain of all the disarray and disarray that keep you from thinking obviously. Your psychological lucidity is basic for assuming responsibility for your fate. Perception, then again, gives an impulse

to show your enthusiastic longings for well-being, achievement, and flourishing in all aspects of your life.

Be Of Good Cheer: Do not view life in a serious way. Figure out how to chuckle

notwithstanding your hardships of life and transform your challenges into perfect occasions. Giggling alleviates your difficulties and perks you up; it is a superb method for destroying your downturn while filling you, keeping in mind the desire for the more brilliant days to come.

Become a close acquaintance with Your Difficulties: Your experiences are not intended to break you however act as illustrations of life for

the headway of your otherworldly development. All troubles are temporary; they come quickly into your life and vanish whenever you have managed them. Consequently, get to know your hardships and change them into perfect circumstances without grappling with them.

Avoid Negative People: Maintain your distance truly, intellectually, and genuinely from critical attitudes. They have a terrible impact on your mind and will continuously put you in your way to progress and bliss down. These have zero desire to rise and will ruin others also from progressing on the way to success.

Reformat Your Subconscious With Affirmations: Break

liberated from your old, behaving destructively convictions and impart useful idea designs with positive confirmations. Confirmations assist with making groundbreaking insight designs that are favorable for your own and profound turn of events. The strong assertions, when recited with confidence and enthusiasm, are significantly viable in assisting you with accomplishing your objectives effectively.

Know about Your Thoughts: Use your cognizant attention to keep a mind for your psychological exercises. Be aware of your viewpoints at some random time. Your cognizant mindfulness goes about as a protection from the meddling

contemplations that weaken the brain. At the point when you wind up engaging in some bad thought which upsets your internal harmony, supplant it promptly with that which makes you cheerful and splendid. With training, your psyche will eventually be adjusted to abiding in the radiance of idealism.

Charter 2

Create Vision For Yourself

What is an individual vision explanation?

For what reason is it vital to have one?

What must an individual vision explanation have?

A few inquiries to pose to yourself before drafting your vision proclamation

4 moves toward composing an individual vision proclamation

Set it up as a regular occurrence

Our lives and professions are an intricate blend of components. Now and then we feel unfit to be mindful of everything. Some of the time, we feel like we ought to begin once again throughout everyday life. An individual vision proclamation can help when we don't know how things are associated.

We feel unfit to take care of everything around us when we don't know what our motivation is at the point at which we do what we are doing. A dream explanation can help explain your whys and can provide you

with a feeling of importance and course. What is an individual vision proclamation? "There is no ideal breeze for the mariner who doesn't have any idea where to go". - Seneca, I sec. Promotion

Envision you can find a compass that tells you definitively where you need to go. You can undoubtedly pick either a certain something or another, because of this uncommon device. This sounds perfect, right? Furthermore, this is a precisely exact thing an individual vision explanation does.

An individual vision explanation is an explanation that depicts your qualities, your assets, and your objectives.

It tends to be centered around life or expert

objectives, and situating you toward your drawn-out dreams is planned. It is a device to assist with directing your activities when significant choices must be made or specifically change minutes.

Fruitful individuals regularly survey their vision explanation to get an internal compass, and satisfaction, and to happily experience their days more.

For what reason is it critical to have one?

Research has demonstrated the way that an individual vision explanation can assist with people passing from a pattern of pressure to one of more equilibrium.

At the point when you are in a condition of pressure, you have no clue of control of what's going on in your

life/profession and response-based conduct. Conversely, when you move into a more adjusted state, you have a feeling of internal control about what's going on in your life.

In a condition of equilibrium, we sense we're carrying on with a day-to-day existence and a vocation that are the result of choices that we have made over the long haul. There is a rationale to it. This doesn't mean we have command over the outcomes. There are generally outer conditions that affect us. Nonetheless, this implies that we are the proprietor of our reactions. On the off chance that these reactions are adjusted to what our identity is and to our qualities, we

have a feeling of satisfaction and satisfaction.

The following are 5 explicit advantages that come from having an individual vision proclamation:

It becomes more straightforward to decide.

On the off chance that you wind up in a specific snapshot of your life or vocation in which significant and complex choices should be made, having an individual vision explanation can be a compass for you. It will help you to remember your inward characteristics, values, and purposes that will assist you with distinguishing the best way for you.

It furnishes you with an internal compass.

We, as people, need to feel that what we are doing (in our lives and work) has meaning. To find inspiration for activities, we want to know that what we are doing is commendable and that will drive us someplace. An individual assertion associated with your vision offers to you a feeling of where you are going and of what you need to accomplish.
It assists you with deciding your long-haul and momentary objectives.
This ability to know east from the west can be separated into long haul and momentary objectives. After making your assertion, you will have an unmistakable long-haul objective that will assist you with defining momentary objectives and

significant stages to accomplish it. The drawn-out objective will for the most part stay stable consistently and will illuminate transient objectives that will change over the long haul.

It will furnish you with inspiration during difficult stretches.

At the point when times become hard, it is challenging to keep up with inspiration and continue taking care of your business or putting resources into your existence with energy. Having a composed assertion can assist you with helping yourself to remember your whys and welcome you into the groove again.

It will assist you with carrying on with a healthy lifestyle.

An elegantly composed assertion contains

various parts of your life both individual and expert, profound and step-by-step situated. Helping yourself to remember your assertion will assist you with carrying on with a more healthy lifestyle.

What must an individual vision proclamation have?

A very much framed individual vision proclamation needs to answer these inquiries: what is it that you need to do? Why? How might you do that? You might need to think about your qualities, assets, and abilities to choose your objectives. Taking into account these will offer significant understanding about your whys and how you do what others do another way.

An individual vision proclamation ought to contain:

Your inclinations

What are you enthusiastic about? A dream proclamation ought to contain your inclinations and interests, what you appreciate doing in your leisure time, and what you would do the entire day on the off chance that you didn't need to work.

Your abilities

A very much shaped assertion ought to incorporate what you are great at. It can incorporate proficient and individual abilities in light of your perceptions and criticism got through years from relatives, companions, and associates.

Your qualities

What are you driven by? A strong assertion illuminates your driving qualities. They are normally communicated in a general structure (like love, imagination, equity) and are those qualities without which life (for you) has neither rhyme nor reason.

What the world requirements

What is it that the world needs, as you would like to think? The solution to this question ought to be essential for your assertion since it educates something concerning what is significant for yourself and what can significantly impact everybody.

Your objective

If you know what your identity is, what drives you, and what the world necessities, you are

prepared to recognize your life/profession objective. This is the very thing that the Japanese way of thinking addresses as ikigai, which is a drawn-out objective adjusted to every one of the areas above. Your ikigai can furnish you with a feeling of direction and course. Certain individuals consider it live's motivation.

A few inquiries to pose to yourself before drafting your vision proclamation

Making an individual vision proclamation can be a seriously thoughtful work. Saving 10 minutes of reflection before drafting can assist with explaining your thoughts and jump quickly into the 4-step process you'll track down the made sense of in the following section.

Here, you'll discover a few significant inquiries to direct your appearance and groundwork for the production of the assertion. If you are more activity arranged, you can bounce into the 4-step cycle and utilize these inquiries depending on the situation.

What have you done since you were a kid that provides you with a great deal of fulfillment?

In which exercises do you feel completely stimulated?

What are you great at?

Without which values (min 3 - max 6) does life have neither rhyme nor reason?

What is it that the world needs?

How might you want to be recollected toward the finish of your days?

As indicated by your past responses, what could be a daily existence/profession objective which sounds good to you?

4 moves toward composing an individual vision proclamation

This 4-step process is something I made after very nearly 10 years of involvement with over 100 exceptionally capable representatives being developed focuses meant to assist them with characterizing an objective and fostering their true capacity. This is a proof put together interaction based on notable clinicians and scientists (most importantly: sensible levels by Robert Dilts, grateful request by

Positive Psychology, and Bob Proctor's visioning cycle).

The whole interaction requires around 40 minutes of reflection. Preferably, every one of the means is done together, yet breaking reflection into stages will not hinder the interaction.

Stage 1: Letter from what's in store

This is a stage where you can let your creative mind go and your imagination stream.

Envision yourself being 90 years of age, and has carried on with a fantasy existence with a truly amazing line of work.

Take a piece of paper and a pen and compose a letter to you of today representing things to come. Portray all that you have achieved in your own life and work,

how these achievements cause you to feel, and what you are generally glad for.

Stage 2: List of accomplishments

What do you characterize as progress? Get some margin to consider 4 accomplishments in your day-to-day existence. They can be something individual (get hitched, have a kid) or expert (get advanced, get another line of work). Preferably, you'll need to incorporate both. Portray your victories, how you have caused them to turn out to be genuine and why they apply to you.

Stage 3: Collecting information

In this step, we need to gather the two components from the letter from the future and the rundown of

achievements. Peruse both once more and circle watchwords that have to do with the accompanying fields: climate, abilities, feelings, convictions, values, and reason.

Climate: it alludes to all that has to do with the climate you imagined (warmth, steady...).

Abilities: they allude to capabilities, for example, critical thinking, direction, inventiveness, etc.

Feelings: they connect with the profound setting. You can probably discover a few feelings portrayed in your letter (euphoria, fulfillment, and so forth... .).

Convictions: these are your considerations communicated in an overall manner, for instance, "when I

buckle down, I accomplish what I need" or "when I ask individuals they support me."

Values: they are widespread driving qualities like love, consideration, equity, etc.

Reason: it connects with your main goal. You might find it communicated as a response to the inquiry: how would you like to affect the planet?

Stage 4: Writing down your vision explanation (6 minutes)

Presently you have every one of the watchwords to record your vision proclamation. On the off chance that you are a visual individual, you could make a drawing with these watchwords, however, it is prescribed to have it in

a composed structure as well. For the vision explanation to be powerful, it ought to be basically as nitty gritty as you can make it.

If this is the initial time endeavoring this activity, it very well may be trying to envision how an assertion ought to be shaped. Here you can discover a few models

Chapter 3

Build a Better Habit For Wealth and Health

10 Habits to Help You Be Healthy, Wealthy, and Wise This Year

These tips will assist you with amplifying your life this year

It tends to be invigorating to begin once more. You might have that internal push to do more this year.

You are not set in stone to carry on with a superior life.

To utilize that inspiration, you ought to assemble the appropriate propensities and dispose of the awful ones.

"Today, be appreciative and think about how rich you are. Your family is invaluable, your time is gold, and your wellbeing is abundant."

The following are 10 propensities that could be useful to you carry on with a solid, well-off, and savvy life.

1. Stand More

Assuming that you have an Apple Watch, it suggests you represent 12 hours consistently. Standing is crucial to your well-being.

Research has found that individuals who sit for a

long time consistently have a more prominent possibility of diabetes, coronary illness, and kicking the bucket prior throughout everyday life. To assist you with standing more over the day, utilize a standing work area.

A standing work area isn't a pattern; it assists us with beating our stationary way of life.

A standing work area assists you with decreasing the time you spend on your seat. It has many advantages, including working on your state of mind, expanding your energy level, and consuming more calories.

Key Takeaway

Standing more is a fundamental way of life change that can work on your physical and mental wellbeing. Put resources into a

standing work area since it can assist you with lessening corpulence, decrease back torment, and transform lethargy into efficiency.

2. Get Enough Sleep

"Without enough rest, we as a whole become tall 2-year-olds." — JoJo Jensen, an entertainer

You may not understand you are not getting sufficient rest, but rather your body offers you cautioning hints. Try not to wear the identification of pride that you are not getting sufficient rest. Rest is basic to your well-being and everyday execution.

Rest isn't exaggerated.

Try not to accept others when they say they don't require rest since they are social, occupied, and courageous. An absence of rest is

something terrible, not something to be thankful for. Try not to figure you can get up ahead of schedule and hit the hay late. It will find you.

Rest causes us more useful and empowers us to feel stimulated and alert. As indicated by the National Sleep Foundation, most sound grown-ups need 7 to 9 hours of rest an evening (rest necessities fluctuate marginally from one individual to another). Rest assists you with controlling your weight, works on your long haul and momentary memory, and forestalls cardiovascular infections.

Key Takeaway

Getting sufficient rest consistently empowers our bodies to fix, decrease pressure and

lifts our safe frameworks.

3. Rest More

"Great wellbeing is valid riches." — Urijah Faber, an American blended military craftsman

You can get eight hours of rest, and you can in any case feel tired. Rest is about your body, while rest is about your psyche. You reestablish your psyche, feelings, and social prosperity when you rest.

Rest and rest are unique.

Rest is tied in with dealing with your brain. It can improve your efficiency since you have a superior feeling of what your identity is and assist you with defeating depletion. There are five distinct sorts of rest you want.

Key Takeaway

Rest is unique about rest. It would be best for

your well-being assuming you get sufficient rest and rest in your life.

4. Practice More

"Deal with your body. It's the main spot you need to live." — Jim Rohn, an American business visionary

Most grown-ups don't practice 30 minutes per day. As indicated by the U.S. Branch of Health and Human Services, grown-ups ought to get no less than 150 minutes every seven days of moderate oxygen-consuming movement or 75 minutes per seven-day stretch of overwhelming high-impact action. Customary activity helps your temperament, bliss, and uplifting perspective on life.

Practice makes you more joyful than cash does.

Research has observed that ordinary activity is more fundamental to your emotional well-being than the amount of cash you possess. The practice assists you with dozing better, beating sadness, and lessening pressure. Focus on practice and an everyday propensity.

Key Takeaway

The most joyful individuals in life are the ones who reliably sort out, not get the most cash flow.

5. Center around a Healthy Diet

"No medication can beat a healthy lifestyle." — Benjamin Franklin, principal architect of the United States

For getting healthy, the kind of food you eat is everything. At the point

when you work on your eating regimen, you increment your life expectancy and have quick medical advantages.
Center around what you eat and pay attention to your body. Use food as a chance to be appreciative of your life.
Pick entire food sources over exceptionally handled food varieties. Entire food sources contain fewer calories and are more filling than handled food sources.
Be aware of what you put into your body.
Smart dieting is essential to great well-being.
You can have a solid eating regimen by staying away from sodas, eating more leafy foods, and eating eggs, fish, and nuts. Bring down how much sugar

is in your eating regimen. Either eat less or practice more or both.

Key Takeaway

You'll have a superior memory, be feeling better, and get more fit when you center around a sound eating regimen.

6. Go with Better Decisions

"At times the littlest choices can change your life always." — Keri Russell, an American entertainer

Our choices influence all aspects of our lives. Your decisions consistently develop over the long haul, and they figure out who you become and what kind of daily routine you experience today.

Life is brimming with decisions, and there are numerous awkward bits of insight about existence that we should

acknowledge. A few choices in life are simple, while some are hard.

Our decisions affect progress and disappointment.

The key is to pursue better decisions consistently. Life gives us many crossroads. At the point when you pursue better decisions, your future self will be much obliged.

Our lives are brief minutes with numerous choices. Stand firm on your choices and realize that it was the best decision at that point.

Key Takeaway

To go with better decisions, center around the now, improve and contemplate the drawn-out benefits. Life is difficult and fair, so the little decisions in life go quite far.

7. Fortify Your Relationships

You presumably have associations with family, companions, and partners. In any case, how profound would they say they are? In all likelihood, you are simply on a glimpse of something larger. Pose explicit inquiries to extend your connections.

Connections in your own and proficient life are fundamental to your prosperity. Be interested in them. You might have known somebody for quite a long time, yet you don't have the foggiest idea about certain things about their life since they haven't had the potential chance to impart them to you.

"What's in the store has a place with the

inquisitive." — Anonymous

Research says when you have strong connections at work, you are more drawn in, produce great work, and are all the more truly and sincerely solid. Your connections matter, particularly working, since 33% of your life is spent working.

Key Takeaway

At the point when you strive to assemble more significant connections, you'll become more joyful. To make a real association, don't regard an individual as an exchange, show interest, and listen more than you talk.

8. Contribute More Time with Family

"The key is in not investing energy, but rather in money management." — Stephen R. Brood, an

American teacher, creator, finance manager, and featured expert

Contribute time with individuals who truly make a difference to you. Assuming you just had one day to live, who might you adore? It's likely your loved ones. Be particular about who you invest energy with and treasure the notable individuals in your day-to-day existence.

Your time ought to match your qualities. Self-reflect and ask yourself: the main thing, what do I truly think often about, and what's my motivation?

That self-reflection will in all probability assist you with understanding that you ought to invest more energy with family. Have one dinner together for seven days.

Take a walk together. Plan a pleasant action together. Switch off innovation, play a tabletop game, and get to realize them better.

Perhaps one of your relatives was a beekeeper before throughout everyday life, and you didn't have the foggiest idea. You are shocked that you have hardly any familiarity with your family when you put forth a genuine attempt to get to know them and pay attention to stories you never heard.

Key Takeaway

Achievement breeds achievement, so be fussy about who you invest energy with during your life. Your family presumably positions at the top.

9. Have a Growth Mindset

A development mentality centers around the cycle and the stuff to succeed. On the off chance that you don't have the right outlook, you can't improve as you. The brain is a strong "muscle" that approaches your encounters throughout everyday life.

A development outlook assists you with focusing on learning over the disappointment, greatness over flawlessness, and dangers over business as usual. You view disappointments as any open doors, and you change your attitude toward your life.

Research shows your mind influences your life expectancy. A development mentality

can defeat troublesome and difficult things.

Having a legitimate point of view on everyday routine will decide how you experience your life.

At the point when you approach what is happening as an opportunity for growth and learning experience, you can carry on with a full life.

Key Takeaway

You change your life when you alter your perspective. A development outlook will assist you with seeing the positive in all things. Your psyche is a strong aspect of you and empowers you to adapt and beat difficult stretches.

10. Giggle More

"Continuously giggle when you can. It is a modest medication." —

Lord Byron, a British Romantic writer

A large number of us are focused on as far as possible. Giggling is one of the most outstanding ways of decreasing our pressure. It is an incredible asset to work on your physical and mental wellbeing. Research has observed that giggling is a superb method for alleviating pressure in your life.

Giggling is the perfect thing for you.

Giggling helps various regions of your cerebrum, and it has many advantages that help your wellbeing. Track down ways of giggling consistently, for example, spending time with family, companions, and partners who make you snicker or watch your #1 professional comic.

Key Takeaway

Giggling is free medication. It can assist with away focusing on and tension. That is quite serious!

Uniting It All

This year, there are 10 propensities to assist you with being solid, rich, and shrewd. Stand, rest, and exercise more. Get sufficient rest, center around a solid eating routine, and pursue better decisions. Fortify your connections, contribute additional time with family, have a development mentality, an

Chapter 4

Unveiling your inner greatness

Have you at any point thought about how another profoundly fruitful individual can

assist you with diverting your internal significance to marvelous achievement? Would you like to reach out with your own inward significance?

Regular and all around the world individuals are doing astonishing things. There are individuals who have dominated their interests and who are accomplishing a few great outcomes. Logically there is a specialist who is doing precisely the exact thing you would need to do at the present time.

These individuals are not godlike or some way or another inaccessible, but instead they do regular things and have systems that you can figure out how to find success also.

Here are the 6 stages that you can take for uncovering your internal significance:

1. Characterize precisely very thing you need

Frequently individuals have no clue about what they need throughout everyday life and they are hopeless as a result of it. The initial step is to characterize precisely the exact thing it is that you need. At the point when you clarify the thing you are pursuing your psyche has a clear objective as a main priority that it can go for and move you towards. As a rule karma or occurrence will simply seem to give you the open doors you want.

"There is one quality which one should have to win, and that is definiteness of direction, the

information on what one needs, and a deep yearning to have it." - Napoleon Hill

2. Figure out who has done it before you

The key is to explore and get a comprehension of who has really done what you believe that you should do in life as opposed to individuals who simply discuss it. Take as much time as is needed to get a decent comprehension of the specialists who have some familiarity with turning into the individual you need to turn into. Select your master cautiously. See as the best. Ask yourself, "Could I truly need to turn out to be very much like this individual?"

3. Assimilate this master's all's happy

Whether it is a YouTube channel, a blog, or any free satisfaction that your master has, begin there and ingest every last bit of it. You need to consume as much data conceivable from this instructor of yours so you can discover this individual's internal mentalities as well as how they obtain astonishing outcomes.
You need to go for the gold instructor's smartest understudy. You will definitely know that individual's ideas and thoughts prior to happening to a higher level.
4. Bring the master into your life
On the off chance that you can be companions with the master or could have them as a mentor I would profoundly empower doing as such. Colossal

development can happen when you get a mentor or line up with positive impacts who can push you higher than ever.
At the point when you get a mentor or guide they will actually want to show you new things, yet more significantly they can take you to a more significant level of reasoning and they will push you to turn out to be far superior.
Frequently when you are seeking after this new ability you will draw in new companions and individuals into your life who are pursuing exactly what you need. This is an astounding chance to become friends with the individual who has what it takes you are searching for.

5. Go learn something contrarily related

Testing the entirety of your freshly discovered information and abilities with something inconsistent yet still related will be the test that moves you considerably further. Two everyday issues like connections and blended combative techniques, or power lifting and significantly improving at business is the means by which you can relate this one.

This is significant so you will at first see these subjects as totally unique and irrelevant, however soon you will track down that the vital fundamental standards for having outcome in one region will lead you to progress in this new region.

By dominating more subjects that don't

appear to be connected you will wind up developing considerably more in your insight and use of your most memorable range of abilities.

6. Show your ability in the first art to other people

Likely the main thing that you can do to drive yourself to be a specialist regarding any matter is to go out and instruct regarding that matter.

At the point when you show others your insight you must be a specialist. Moreover you put forth a concentrated effort with the fundamentals, permitting yourself to revisit your own way of learning to instruct it to other people. This permits you to go further in all the information that you

have procured regarding the matter.

At the point when you show your recently discovered expertise and information to others it will lead you to significantly encourage movement of drawing out your internal significance.

"You can have everything in life you need, assuming that you will simply assist others with getting what they need."

Conclusion

Your fate is a vital part of your life that you shouldn't underestimate, the previous you begin pursuing your predetermination the better for you, your present will tell a greater amount of how

your Destiny will seem to be, change your current now, plan how you believe that you predetermination should seem to be and make progress toward you imagined predetermination.

www.ingramcontent.com/pod-product-compliance
Lightning Source LLC
LaVergne TN
LVHW052102160826
845678LV00015B/3317

* 9 7 9 8 8 4 4 3 7 0 0 6 9 *